300 WINNING LOTTERY AFFIRMATIONS

*Affirmations to Win the Lottery
With the Law of Attraction*

written by

EDDIE CORONADO

If you have read my other books you know that the Law of Attraction always responds to persistent, committed action. It does so because it is an eternal, spiritual law that is impartial and universal. This means that it will respond to anyone who uses it correctly. And because this power is infinite you can use it to manifest anything you desire, including millions of dollars. In fact, throughout the years many people have used the Law of Attraction to win contests, sweepstakes, and even lottery jackpots. The common denominator among every lottery winner who has manifested a winning ticket is that they were committed to using positive affirmations every day until their desire became their reality. They understood the immense power of their spoken word, and they used it to transform their lives and circumstances. This book will inspire you to do the same.

WHY YOU SHOULD READ THIS BOOK

This book contains 300 of the most powerful affirmations for manifesting lottery prizes. These affirmations have been used by several lottery winners to win prizes ranging from $50,000.00 to several million dollars. The affirmations in this book are designed to give you a winning edge because they were written to inspire you, awaken your hope, and empower you to manifest the prosperity and abundance you deserve. There are no limits to the amount of money you can manifest with the Law of Attraction. The only limits you have are those within your consciousness, and those limiting beliefs can be changed through the persistent use of positive affirmations. This book provides all the tools you will need to manifest your desires with the power of your spoken word. Once you transform your beliefs and expectations, all the wonderful things you desire will become a part of your life.

WHAT THIS BOOK CONTAINS

This book begins with a Question and Answer Section that covers several of the most important questions about the effective use of affirmations. In addition to learning how to develop the habit of using affirmations daily, you will learn the best time to repeat affirmations, how often you should repeat them, how long it will take to change your beliefs, and a lot of other practical information. You will also learn how to harness the power of your spoken word through the use of two rarely used manifestation tools that can be used to increase your prosperity. In addition, you will learn how to double the effectiveness of your affirmations by incorporating a very important element that is often forgotten by most people who use them. After you read the Question and Answer Section, you will find 300 lottery affirmations that will provide you with a powerful, winning edge. By the time you finish reading this book you will be equipped with the tools necessary to transform your life with the dynamic power of your spoken word.

QUESTION AND ANSWER SECTION

Affirmations and how to use them effectively

The following section covers some of the most important questions that relate to using affirmations to win lottery prizes. Keep in mind that words, in themselves, are not powerful. Words are tools that can be used to generate positive feelings, which are very powerful and creative. Everything you manifest will be the result of the positive feelings you emit like a powerful magnetic frequency. As a result, it is very important that you strive to feel positive and expectant as much as possible as you focus on winning money with the Law of Attraction. Manifesting wealth is not a matter of wishful thinking. It is based on an eternal, unfailing spiritual law that responds to everyone because the Law of Attraction is impersonal and non-judgmental. This immense power is set in motion through your beliefs and feelings. A good question to ask as you repeat affirmations is, "How am I feeling right now?" If you are not feeling positive and expectant, then make up your mind to feel good as you repeat your affirmations. Through commitment and practice, you will gradually transform the way you feel while repeating your affirmative statements. The positive feelings you generate will increase your expectation, and when that happens your desire will become a part of your life.

QUESTION: Can I write my own lottery affirmations?

ANSWER: Yes, you can and should write some of your own affirmations if you feel inspired to do so. Once you have written a number of affirmations that feel right, you can use them with the affirmations in this book. The key to success is to use statements that make you feel positive and expectant. You cannot expect your affirmations to work if you don't feel good while repeating them. This is why it is so important to choose words and ideas that inspire you. As you repeat your affirmations, the positive feelings you generate will align you to the things and conditions you desire. The key to writing effective affirmations is to compose short statements that get right to the point. An affirmation that is too long is not as effective as an affirmation that gets to the point, such as, "I am blessed with good fortune" or "I am destined to win a big lottery jackpot." So keep this in mind as you create your own lottery affirmations. In the meantime, you can use the affirmations in this book until you feel inspired to write some of your own. You should always strive to use affirmations that inspire you whether or not you have written them.

QUESTION: How often should I repeat my lottery affirmations?

ANSWER: You should repeat your affirmations as often as possible throughout the day. Keep in mind that the purpose of repeating affirmations is to build your belief that the things and conditions you desire are on the way to you. Read through the affirmations in this book and create a list of your favorites. Once you have compiled this list, you should commit to using a handful of affirmations each week. Beginning each morning, repeat your affirmations before getting out of bed. Upon awakening, your mind is very fertile and open to suggestions. This is the perfect time to begin repeating affirmations because you will experience little or no internal resistance when affirming at this time. This habit will set the tone of your morning and it will be easier for you to create and maintain a positive attitude throughout the day. As you go about your day, you should consider repeating your affirmations whenever you have the time, such as while showering, while walking your dog, while washing dishes, or while driving to and from work. If you don't have the privacy to speak affirmations aloud, then you should repeat them mentally or write them on a pad of paper, but always strive to fill your mind with positive thoughts and feelings about the things you desire. You cannot expect to manifest your desires if you are not committed to focusing on them in thought, words, feelings and actions. You must give attention to your intention by thinking about what you want and feeling the way you would feel if your desires were already a part of your life. Affirmations will help you feel good about the things you desire, and as you maintain these positively charged feelings you will soon discover that the events of your life will take the form of your thoughts, feelings, words and expectations. Finally, another great idea is to repeat your affirmations in the evening just before drifting off to sleep. Your mind is fertile and open to suggestions as it enters the restful theta brain wave state, which is a perfect time to impregnate the subconscious mind with the suggestion that you can win the lottery with the Law of Attraction. Many people who repeat these affirmations prior to sleep have reported having vivid dreams about winning the lottery and they wake up feeling excited about manifesting their desire. A friend from Oakland, California, who won a large Mega Millions prize, told me that she never fails to repeat her affirmations at night before falling asleep. As a result of her commitment to affirmations, she often has vivid dreams about her desires and she regularly wakes up feeling excited and positive about manifesting money. Her positive feelings and expectation has allowed her to live a happy, prosperous life in which she enjoys peace of mind, world travel, and all the money she needs to enjoy her life and family.

QUESTION: How can I make my spoken affirmations more effective?

ANSWER: Once you have created a list of affirmations that empower you, you should focus on repeating them feelingly, which will make your affirmations even more powerful. For example, if you repeat the affirmation "I am a powerful money magnet," you should strive to feel the way you would feel if you were rich and prosperous. How would you feel to have an endless supply of money to enjoy? How would you feel knowing that you have complete financial freedom? Think about how you would feel to be in this position, and then incorporate these wonderful feelings into your affirmation exercises. When you feel exactly what you would feel to have your desires right now, you are affirming that you have what you want and your positive feelings are placing you in alignment with everything you desire. On the other hand, when you are longing for something and thinking about what you don't have, you are emitting the frequency of not having it. As a result, your negative energy is attracting more of not having it. This is why it is so important to monitor all your thoughts and feelings when manifesting your desires.

The Universe responds to the way you feel, so you should always strive to feel good about the things and conditions you desire. You can literally transform your life by changing your words and feelings.

QUESTION: Once I begin using affirmations, how long will it take to change my beliefs and expectations?

ANSWER: After a few weeks you should start noticing a change in the way you feel about your ability to manifest money with the Law of Attraction, but don't be disappointed if it takes a bit longer. As you persist in declaring what you want, you will soon discover that the events and circumstances of your life will change: doors will open, opportunities will present themselves, pleasant surprises will greet you at every turn, and the money you have will last longer. Most importantly, you will feel like a winner, and the positive feelings you emit will place you in alignment with all the wonderful things you desire. As a result, you should persist in declaring exactly what you want to show up in your life. When working with the Law of Attraction, you must understand that there is no one to change but yourself. You are not begging an external divine power to answer your prayers. You are recognizing your divine connection to the Infinite Spirit of God and allowing it to work through your life. You are a part of the Infinite Spirit and it is a part of you. As a result, the only way you can create the life of your dreams is through a change in consciousness. When you change your beliefs and expectations, your experiences in life will change. This is why it is so important to persist in repeating your affirmations and imagining what you would do if your dreams were your reality right now. The Universe loves persistence and it will reward you generously for it.

QUESTION: Should I monitor all my words as I focus on manifesting my desires?

ANSWER: Yes, it is very important to be mindful of everything you say as you focus on manifesting what you want. You cannot expect to win the lottery if you affirm positive statements for fifteen minutes and then spend the rest of your day talking about lack and limitation. Your words have the power to influence your feelings, and your feelings emit a powerful frequency that attracts the events and conditions of your life. If your words are negative, then your frequency will be negative and the corresponding results will be undesirable. This is why it is important to be aware of all your words, especially your casual conversations. Don't ever joke or talk negatively about your financial situation or those of another person. Be positive about everything you think, say and feel, and you will soon discover that the events of your life will take on the tone of your positive thoughts and feelings. It might be a challenge at first, but it will become easier with practice. Also, don't get discouraged if you occasionally slip up with a negative word or make a negative statement. Nobody is perfect, and we all miss the mark from time to time. The important thing is to recognize your weak points, learn from them, and then commit to incorporating positive words, thoughts, feelings and actions into every aspect of your life.

QUESTION: Can I really use the Law of Attraction to win the lottery?

ANSWER: People have been using the Law of Attraction to win lottery prizes for many years. In fact, some people have won several lottery and casino jackpots using the creative power of intention. Throughout the years I have interviewed a number of people who have manifested jackpots ranging from fifty thousand dollars to several million dollars. Each person interviewed said that his or her jackpot was the result of using positive affirmations on a daily basis. In fact, many of these prize winners repeated their positive affirmations several dozen times per day and constantly monitored their thoughts and feelings, as well. As one Law of Attraction lottery winner told me, "You cannot expect to manifest millions of dollars if you say negative things and feel negatively all day long." As a result, when working with the Law of Attraction it is very important to feel good as often as possible. Your words influence the way you feel, and the way you feel influences how the Law of Attraction responds to you, so you should use your words thoughtfully and align to your positive affirmations by saying positive things and feeling good even when you are not repeating your affirmations. You can easily cancel the effectiveness of your affirmations by saying something negative, gossiping, arguing with someone, or by rehashing negative memories and feelings of the past. In a nutshell, you should commit to staying on target by speaking positive words and by feeling good as much as possible throughout the day. If you do so, the Universal Law will reward your efforts. You are working with a spiritual law that has no choice but to respond to your thoughts, feelings and expectations. If you put in the positive effort, you will begin to see positive results. It's as simple as that.

QUESTION: Are affirmations more effective than visualization exercises?

ANSWER: Affirmations and visualization exercises are equally effective because each of these manifestation tools has the potential to make you feel good about manifesting your desires. You will know which manifestation tool is best for you based on how they make you feel. If you can become emotionally stimulated by repeating positive affirmations, then you should use affirmations as much as possible throughout the day. In general, affirmations are easier to use because you can literally use them anywhere and at any time. For example, you can repeat your affirmations while driving, cleaning the house or walking the dog. Visualization exercises, on the other hand, require more concentration because these exercises are generally done while you are sitting with your eyes closed. In addition, spoken words have the power to quickly influence the way you feel. If you need inspiration, for example, you might decide to use an affirmation that is filled with words that encourage you to feel positive, hopeful and expectant. A friend from California, for example, uses the following affirmation when she needs a boost in her faith. She repeats, "If the Law of Attraction has worked for others, it will work for me, too!" She also affirms, "All my words are incredibly powerful, so I use them wisely." She said that the use of these affirmations has encouraged her to persist in manifesting her desires when many other people have given up. She enjoys the way she feels while repeating affirmations, so she maintains a growing list of her favorites. She repeats her affirmations throughout the day as she cleans her room, exercises, and tends to her garden. As a result of her commitment, she has manifested many wonderful things, including a better paying job with medical benefits and a pension, a new car, and a fiancé who is a prosperous businessman. She is now a very prosperous woman who credits her success to her commitment to the Law of Attraction. During a phone call one evening, she said to me, "I transformed my entire life through the power of my spoken word."

QUESTION: What should I do if I feel uninspired or lazy at times?

ANSWER: It's natural to feel uninspired or lazy once in a while, but it's important to remain committed to repeating your affirmations each day no matter how you feel. This is especially true in the beginning as you commit to building a positive habit. Most of the time you will feel enthusiastic about using the power of your spoken word, but occasionally you might feel frustrated or tired after a long day at work. If this is the case, you should have a cup of green tea, take a walk, or do something that helps you unwind. Once you feel more relaxed, you should begin repeating the affirmations that encourage you to feel good about manifesting your desires. Through persistence you will develop a habit that is enjoyable and easy to practice on a daily basis. In the beginning, you should commit to repeating affirmations for five minutes per day. Once you have become accustomed to this five-minute habit, you should increase your affirmation time to ten or fifteen minutes per day as long as it's a reasonable amount of time. You cannot expect to develop a positive habit by committing to long stretches of time, especially in the beginning when you are still learning. Start small, then increase your affirmations time as you learn what works and as you begin to associate positive feelings with your affirmations. Eventually, you will discover that fifteen minutes per day is a breeze. There are many people who repeat their affirmations twice a day, fifteen minutes each time. The amount of time you spend repeating affirmations is not as important as how you feel when and after you repeat them. If you feel good after affirming for ten or fifteen minutes, then you are on the right track and all the wonderful things you desire will come into your life as a result of your evolving consciousness. The key to success is to persist until your words feel true. When this happens, you will discover that the events and circumstances of your life will be an exact reflection of your words, thoughts, feelings and expectations.

QUESTION: What is an Intention Statement and how can I use it to manifest lottery prizes?

ANSWER: As mentioned in my book titled ADVANCED LAW OF ATTRACTION TECHNIQUES, an Intention Statement is one of the most powerful Law of Attraction tools you will ever use to manifest your desires. An Intention Statement, when used regularly, can literally cut your manifestation time in half. Although many authors have written about the creative power of affirmations, many have failed to explain what an Intention Statement is and how to use it effectively. In a nutshell, an Intention Statement is a concise statement that describes the things and conditions you desire. If you want to become financially prosperous your Intention Statement might be similar to the following statement, "MY INTENTION IS TO BE FINANCIALLY PROSPEROUS SO I CAN SAVE AT LEAST TWO THOUSAND DOLLARS A MONTH, BUY

EVERYTHING I WANT, AND HAVE THE LIFE OF MY DREAMS." If you want to lose weight by adopting a healthy lifestyle your Intention Statement might be similar to the following statement, "MY INTENTION IS TO LOSE WEIGHT BY EATING HEALTHY FOODS AND EXERCISING EVERY DAY." If you want to manifest a lottery jackpot your Intention Statement might be similar to the following statement: "MY INTENTION IS TO WIN A MULTI-MILLION DOLLAR LOTTERY PRIZE WITHIN A YEAR FROM NOW." The key to writing an effective Intention Statement is to use words and ideas that accurately describe the things and conditions you desire. As you brainstorm for words that best describe your desires, be sure that your finished statement encourages you to feel good when declaring it. When your Intention Statement makes you feel good you will enjoy using it more often and you will produce better results with it. It is important to remember that an Intention Statement is not a magic spell. It helps you give attention to your intention, which is a key to manifestation. And because it only takes a few seconds to say, you should consider repeating your Intention Statement at least three times per day:

morning, noon, and night. As you repeat your Intention Statement, you should imagine that you have exactly what you want and you should focus on feeling exactly how you would feel if your desires were already a part of your life. As you do so, you align yourself to whatever you desire because you are emitting the same frequency of the thing desired. The Law of Attraction is set in motion through the energy and frequency of your thoughts, feelings and expectations, so you should commit to feeling positive and expectant as much as possible.

QUESTION: What's the difference between affirmations and an Intention Statement?

ANSWER: Affirmations are statements that are designed to generate positive and expectant feelings through repetition. For example, if you want to generate positive beliefs and expectations about winning the lottery, you should use a number of affirmations throughout the day such as, "I am focusing all my positive energy on winning the lottery," and "I am a magnet for winning tickets." Although you can and should use a variety of affirmations to build your faith and expectation, you will only use one Intention Statement, such as, "MY INTENTION IS TO WIN A LOTTERY JACKPOT SO BIG THAT I CAN RETIRE EARLY AND LIVE IN LUXURY FOR THE REST OF MY LIFE." Your Intention Statement serves the purpose of clarifying your desire and helps you focus on exactly what you want to show up in your life. Unfortunately, many people fail to take the necessary time to clarify exactly what they want to experience in life because they are too busy with work, family and the demands of life. Thankfully, an Intention Statement is easy to use and only takes a few seconds to say. As a result, there is no excuse for not using an Intention Statement daily. As mentioned previously, it is a good idea to repeat your Intention Statement at least three times per day: morning, noon and night. Your Law of Attraction action plan should include the use of your Intention Statement and whatever positive affirmations you choose to use. Once you have gotten into the habit of using an Intention Statement and positive affirmations each day, you will begin to feel more positive about your desires, and these positive feelings will attract the things and conditions you desire.

QUESTION: In addition to repeating affirmations and using an Intention Statement, is there another practice that will allow me to use the power of my spoken word to speed up my manifestations?

ANSWER: Another powerful practice that will help you harness the tremendous power of your spoken word is to express words of gratitude. In fact, you can speak words of gratitude while you are taking a shower, washing dishes or cleaning your bedroom. The key is to think about all the things you are thankful for and then verbally express gratitude for them. As you are washing dishes or walking your dog you might say, "I am thankful for my job and for my good health," or "I am thankful for my home and all the comforts I enjoy." You might even take a mental inventory of all the things you are thankful for and then express gratitude for your friends, family members, your comfortable bed, or your ability to enjoy a vacation each year. If you live in a constant state of gratitude for everything you have, then you will cultivate and maintain the positive, expectant feelings that are the precursor to manifestation. When you feel good, you create, and gratitude is a wonderful way for you to cultivate positive feelings. Also, be thankful for each and every lottery prize you win along the way, even if you win small prizes in the beginning. Being thankful will help you feel better about everything you have and it will help you attract more wonderful things to be thankful for. A friend in Chicago won several hundred thousand dollars in his state lottery through the daily use of spoken affirmations and gratitude. He was always positive and thankful for every lottery prize he won no matter how small it was. If he won a few dollars, he would express gratitude by saying, "I am thankful for all the lottery prizes that come to me easily and effortlessly. Money constantly flows into my life in great abundance, and I am open and receptive to winning a huge jackpot soon!" Within a few months of implementing a Law of Attraction action plan that included the use of positive affirmations and gratitude, he won a lottery prize so large that it allowed him to pay off his home and retire from work at the age of fifty six.

QUESTION: How many tickets should I buy when I play the lottery?

ANSWER: It's wise to stick with a budget when playing the lottery because winning a jackpot does not require you to buy lots of tickets. In fact, many jackpot winners have admitted to seldom buying more than a few tickets each time they played. As co-creator with the Universe, you should concentrate your positive energy on a few tickets. If you constantly spend lots of money on tickets, your actions are affirming that you must buy several to win. The key to winning the lottery with the Law of Attraction is to create the feeling that you are already a winner. You can accomplish this with the dynamic power of your spoken word. Once this happens, the things and conditions you desire will come to you easily and effortlessly because you will be emitting the same frequency of your desired reality.

"You can transform your entire life by changing your words."

– EDDIE CORONADO

The 300 affirmations in this section will empower you to manifest your lottery jackpot. As you commit to a Law of Attraction action plan that includes spoken affirmations you will quickly learn that your positive, expectant feelings are a necessary ingredient of manifestation. Neville Goddard, a well-known spiritual author and teacher, explained that feelings are the secret of manifestation. In other words, we always attract what we emit in the form of beliefs, feelings and expectations. As a result, you should strive to add feelings to your spoken affirmations whenever you use them. For example, as you repeat the affirmation "I have always known that I would be a lottery winner," you should attempt to feel the joy and excitement that you would feel if you just won millions of dollars in your state lottery. As you repeat your affirmations and emit positive feelings you will move into alignment with all the wonderful things and conditions you desire. Also, it's important to remember that you should strive to feel exactly what you would feel to have your desires right now. Don't over exaggerate your feelings by adding too much emotion or getting too worked up. Instead, focus on feeling exactly what you would feel to be a lottery winner. A good idea is to ask the following questions: How would I feel if I just won a fifty million dollar jackpot? How would I feel to call my best friend with the good news about my big win? How would I feel to have the financial freedom to spend money on anything I want? Once you have become clear about how you would feel to be a lottery millionaire, you should incorporate these feelings into your affirmation exercises. By feeling exactly what you would feel to win the lottery you will attract your desire because you are emitting the frequency of winning. This is what is known as LIKE ATTRACTS LIKE. In working with the Law of Attraction you must keep in mind that you are using an unfailing spiritual law that has no choice but to deliver your desire once you believe and feel that winning the lottery is possible for you.

Another idea to keep in mind is that you will need "luck" to win the lottery with the Law of Attraction, but not luck in the traditional sense of the word. As you harness the tremendous power of your spoken word to create the things and conditions you desire, the word "LUCK" becomes an acronym that takes on an entirely different meaning. The four letters that make up the word "LUCK" now mean "Living Under Cosmic Knowledge." As co-creator with the Universe, you are Living Under Cosmic Knowledge that you have the power to create the events and circumstances of your life through the creative use of your thoughts, feelings, and words. As a result, you should strive to be more thoughtful about everything you say because every word that comes out of your mouth is creative and will eventually return to you in the form of events and circumstances. Simply stated, you have the power to create your own LUCK through the power of your spoken word and your positive expectation.

The following affirmations will help you harness the creative power of your words to manifest lottery prizes. As you use these affirmations, keep in mind that you can substitute the word "lottery" for any game that is offered in your state or country. At the time of this writing, there are many lottery games offered throughout the world, such as Super Lotto Plus, Mega Millions, Powerball, Pick 5, Lotto Max, and several more. Therefore, feel free to use the name of the lottery game that is offered where you live. In addition, you can use some or any of the 300 affirmations in this book, or you can write some of your own affirmations as you build the habit of using them on a daily basis. Keep in mind that words in themselves are not creative, but your feelings behind them are very creative and can be used to transform your life. As you persist in repeating affirmations you will gradually transform your beliefs and expectations, so you should strive to repeat them as often as possible. Also, it's a good idea to read through the list of affirmations and choose a few to use each week. Changing your affirmations regularly will keep it fresh and help you maintain the enthusiasm you need to persist until your desires become manifest.

300 AFFIRMATIONS FOR MANIFESTING LOTTERY PRIZES

Affirmations 1 Through 75

1. Every dollar I play comes back multiplied.

2. I am in the process of manifesting a huge lottery prize.

3. I believe in my ability to win the lottery.

4. I can see myself winning one of the biggest lottery jackpots ever.

5. I deserve to win the lottery.

6. I deserve to have millions of dollars in the bank.

7. I am ready to win a big jackpot.

8. I am open and receptive to winning a huge lottery prize.

9. I believe in my ability to manifest my desires.

10. I know that I will win a lottery jackpot very soon.

11. I have the positive attitude of a lottery winner.

12. I am ready to win the lottery.

13. I am ready to cash in the winning ticket.

14. Winning lots of money comes naturally to me.

15. I have always considered myself a very lucky person.

16. I can clearly imagine myself as a Powerball winner.

17. I am in tune with the financial abundance that is all around me.

18. I believe in my ability to win a huge jackpot.

19. Luck follows me wherever I go.

20. Millions of dollars are coming to me in the form of a lottery prize.

21. Every day I am getting closer to winning a jackpot.

22. I can easily imagine myself cashing in the winning ticket.

23. I feel a big lottery win coming to me.

24. I feel like the luckiest person in the world.

25. Winning the lottery is my destiny.

26. I focus my positive thoughts on winning money.

27. I always buy winning tickets.

28. Winning money comes easily for me.

29. The Universe wants me to be rich.

30. I feel that a big win is about to happen for me.

31. I am excited knowing that I am about to win a jackpot.

32. I am a magnet for winning tickets.

33. It feels wonderful to be a lottery winner.

34. I feel rich today.

35. I will continue to attract winning tickets.

36. Somebody has to win the jackpot, so it might as well be me.

37. I win much more money than I spend.

38. My lottery prizes allow me to have the life of my dreams.

39. I expect to win a jackpot very soon.

40. I look forward to winning multiple lottery prizes.

41. I appreciate my good fortune.

42. I see myself as a millionaire.

43. I am prosperous and wealthy beyond measure.

44. I can use the Law of Attraction to win the lottery.

45. I win enough money to save and invest.

46. I am emitting the powerful frequency of a lottery winner.

47. It is easy for me to attract and maintain my wealth.

48. I am emitting the frequency of wealth.

49. I can feel a big win coming soon.

50. I always imagine myself as a lottery winner.

51. I know that my jackpot is about to manifest for me.

52. My desire to win the lottery is quickly coming to pass.

53. I am comfortable with the thought of winning millions of dollars.

54. I can handle the financial responsibility of being rich.

55. I am open and receptive to the millions of dollars the Universe is sending my way.

56. I know that my lottery jackpot is just around the corner.

57. My intention is to win millions of dollars in my state lottery.

58. Winning lottery prizes comes easily and naturally to me.

59. I have always known that I would be a lottery winner.

60. I am thankful for the financial freedom I have to live the life of my dreams.

61. I enjoy winning money.

62. My positive attitude helps me attract what I want in life.

63. I am financially free thanks to my lottery jackpot.

64. It's exciting to know that I will always be known as a lottery winner.

65. If other people have won the lottery, so can I.

66. I am luckier than anyone I know.

67. I am destined to become an instant millionaire.

68. I am ready to claim my Powerball jackpot.

69. I give myself permission to manifest millions of dollars.

70. I am now attracting my biggest lottery prize.

71. I have the winning edge.

72. I am blessed with good fortune.

73. I spend my lottery prizes wisely and I invest my money.

74. I was meant to be a millionaire.

75. I am determined to win the lottery this year.

Affirmations 76 Through 150

76. I am destined to become rich and prosperous.

77. I can already see and feel the lottery check in my hands.

78. The Law of Attraction will work for anyone who persists with it.

79. I have wonderful plans for my lottery millions.

80. I am brimming with luck and good fortune.

81. I am focusing all my positive energy on winning the lottery.

82. The Universe rewards me for my faith and persistence.

83. Money obeys me when I summon it with the power of my spoken word.

84. The Universe wants me to be rich.

85. I am ready to claim my lottery jackpot this year.

86. I am worthy of having lots of money.

87. There is no lack in the universe, so I focus my intention on becoming a millionaire.

88. I am immersed in positive, winning energy.

89. I am generous with my lottery winnings, but I also save and invest wisely.

90. I have many lottery prizes to be thankful for.

91. It feels wonderful to be rich.

92. My lottery prizes help me achieve great things.

93. I am on the path to winning a huge lottery jackpot.

94. I am manifesting my lottery millions now.

95. The Universe wants me to win the lottery.

96. I am emitting the energy and frequency of a grand prize winner.

97. I feel so thankful that my positive feelings influence everything in my life.

98. The more thankful I am, the more money I attract.

99. Nothing can stop me from winning the lottery.

100. I am happy to see others win because I know it can happen to me, too.

101. Every day that passes brings me closer to winning a lottery jackpot.

102. I can manifest anything I set my heart on, including a big lottery prize.

103. I focus my attention on my intention to win the lottery.

104. I can win as much money as I set my heart on.

105. It's now my turn to win a big lottery jackpot.

106. I know exactly what I will do with my lottery millions.

107. Now that I am a lottery winner I can afford to buy anything I want.

108. It feels wonderful to be a millionaire.

109. I have the amazing ability to pick winning numbers.

110. I truly believe that I can win the lottery.

111. I am destined to win a big lottery jackpot.

112. I believe in my ability to manifest anything I desire.

113. I am attracting a big lottery prize now.

114. Picking the winning numbers comes naturally to me.

115. I always win big lottery prizes.

116. I can easily imagine myself as a lottery winner.

117. I am now using the unfailing Law of Attraction to manifest my lottery millions.

118. My intuition tells me which numbers to play.

119. My words are creative, so I use them to declare myself a lottery winner.

120. Millions of dollars are within my reach.

121. I will take care of my family and friends with my lottery prize money.

122. I am always winning lots of money.

123. My lottery prizes come easily and frequently.

124. I am so thankful for my ability to win the lottery.

125. I win money all the time.

126. It's good to know that I have more money than I can ever spend.

127. Good fortune follows me wherever I go.

128. It's easy to imagine myself winning the lottery.

129. I feel very lucky this week.

130. This is my year to win the lottery.

131. I have faith in my ability to win a big lottery prize.

132. I am ready to claim my jackpot as a lump sum.

133. I am capable of handling large amounts of money.

134. I deserve to win a big Powerball prize.

135. Financial channels are now open, and money flows into my life abundantly.

136. My mind is focused on winning money.

137. I can see myself walking into the lottery office to claim a jackpot.

138. I am mentally prepared to handle millions of dollars in prize money.

139. I will save enough of my lottery winnings so I will never have to work again.

140. I can feel a big lottery prize in my very near future.

141. Nothing can prevent me from manifesting millions of dollars in the lottery.

142. I am focused on manifesting my financial goals.

143. The Universe will reward my persistence by making me a lottery winner.

144. I can easily manifest millions of dollars.

145. The Universe always rewards me with exactly what I focus on attracting.

146. I am totally focused on winning a lottery jackpot.

147. I was meant to be a millionaire.

148. I know exactly what I will do with my lottery prize money.

149. Many people have used the Law of Attraction to win the lottery, and so can I.

150. The positive energy I emit returns to me in the form of winning tickets.

Affirmations 151 Through 225

151. Money miracles happen to me all the time.

152. I am so excited to claim my prize money.

153. Millions of dollars are waiting to be claimed by me.

154. I can already see my name on the lottery check.

155. I can easily imagine millions of dollars in my bank account.

156. Money rushes into my life in great abundance.

157. I attract wealth and abundance with the power of my spoken word.

158. I give myself permission to manifest millions of dollars.

159. I am a powerful money magnet.

160. I have a million dollar mentality that attracts winning tickets.

161. I feel like a lottery millionaire.

162. Winning money comes to me easily and frequently.

163. I have the mindset of a lottery winner.

164. I feel like a lottery jackpot winner today.

165. Money loves me and I love manifesting money.

166. Manifesting money is becoming a normal thing for me.

167. I am about to win a jackpot so big that I could never spend it all.

168. I am worthy of having the life of my dreams.

169. I am open and receptive to millions of dollars in prize money.

170. I am immersed in the powerful energy of luck and good fortune.

171. I can afford anything thanks to my huge lottery payout.

172. I am an irresistible money magnet.

173. It feels wonderful to be a lottery millionaire.

174. I emit the positive frequency of a lottery winner.

175. My intuition is strong, so I use it to pick the winning numbers.

176. Every ticket I buy is a winner.

177. I am now attracting millions of dollars and a fabulous life of luxury.

178. I am a generous lottery winner.

179. My mind emits the frequency of wealth.

180. I know that I will win the lottery this year.

181. I already have big plans for my lottery prize money.

182. I feel positive and expectant every time I buy a lottery ticket.

183. There is a multi-million dollar jackpot in my very near future.

184. I am in the process of manifesting millions of dollars with the Law of Attraction.

185. Money comes to me continually and in great abundance.

186. I have a winning mentality.

187. I am totally focused on winning a huge jackpot.

188. I win lots of money all the time.

189. I feel good about my ability to win the lottery.

190. I give myself permission to be a millionaire.

191. There are no limits to the amount of money I can win in the lottery.

192. I manifest millions of dollars with the dynamic power of my spoken word.

193. I am one with a massive amount of money.

194. I now summon millions of dollars into my life for my joy, comfort and pleasure.

195. I am so thankful for the millions of dollars in my bank account.

196. I can use the Law of Attraction to manifest millions of dollars.

197. I easily attract huge amounts of money.

198. I am grateful for the lottery jackpot I am about to win.

199. I don't have to spend a lot of money to win a lot of money.

200. What I focus on expands, so I focus on winning a lottery jackpot.

201. My ability to attract money increases with every passing day.

202. I feel rich and prosperous today.

203. I am constantly cashing in winning tickets.

204. I am thankful for my ability to manifest as much money as I desire.

205. I am totally aligned with wealth and good fortune.

206. I am a good example that the Law of Attraction works.

207. If the Law of Attraction works for other people, it can work for me.

208. It feels wonderful to know that I will never have to work again.

209. I always have more than enough money thanks to my lottery jackpot.

210. I have the ability to achieve my goal of becoming a lottery millionaire.

211. Nobody deserves to win the lottery more than I do.

212. My biggest lottery prize is about to manifest for me.

213. I have the positive attitude of someone who is about to win millions of dollars.

214. I was born to be a lottery millionaire.

215. I am about to win the biggest lottery prize ever claimed in my state.

216. I am in charge of the way I feel, and today I feel like a millionaire.

217. My thoughts and feelings are focused on winning a huge jackpot.

218. By this time next year I will be a lottery millionaire.

219. There is no limit to the amount of money I can win.

220. It's easy to win millions of dollars.

221. I have faith in my ability to win the lottery with the Law of Attraction.

222. I allow myself to win more money than I ever dreamed possible.

223. All my friends know me as the luckiest person around.

224. I always win money no matter where I buy my tickets.

225. I play the lottery to win big prizes.

Affirmations 226 Through 300

226. I deserve the best in life, including unlimited financial abundance.

227. I choose to think of myself as a lottery millionaire.

228. I now receive the lottery jackpot that is rightfully mine.

229. My spoken word releases avalanches of money into my life.

230. I am so happy to be a lottery millionaire.

231. My desire to win the lottery is manifesting now.

232. My intention is to win a Powerball jackpot very soon.

233. I am thankful for having enough money to buy anything I want, whenever I want.

234. I choose thoughts that make me feel good about winning the lottery.

235. All my dreams are about to come true thanks to my winning ticket.

236. I align with financial abundance by feeling grateful for everything I have.

237. I release all limiting beliefs that interfere with my intention to win the lottery.

238. I expect to win millions of dollars very soon.

239. I am so thankful for the millions of dollars I now have in my bank account.

240. I am now able to help my family and friends with my lottery prize money.

241. My supply of cash is endless thanks to my lottery prize.

242. I have the ability to win more than one jackpot.

243. My source of wealth is my mind.

244. A financial miracle is about to take place in my life.

245. I attract winning tickets easily and effortlessly.

246. My ability to win lottery prizes is unlimited.

247. The Universe wants me to be rich and prosperous.

248. I emit the frequency of a lottery winner, so I only attract winning tickets.

249. My bank account is overflowing with money thanks to my lottery prizes.

250. I know how to manage money, so I will be wise with my lottery millions.

251. I can see myself holding the winning ticket.

252. I always think positively about my ability to win money.

253. I deserve to be rich and prosperous.

254. I am about to win a massive jackpot.

255. The Universe rewards my persistence with lots of money and good fortune.

256. Someone is going to win the lottery, so it might as well be me.

257. Money wants me as much as I want it.

258. I emit the frequency of money, and it flows to me in great abundance.

259. I am capable of spending my prize money wisely so it will last my entire life.

260. My persistent gratitude attracts wealth.

261. My words are creative, so I always talk about myself as a lottery winner.

262. I am thankful for my ability to use the Law of Attraction to manifest money.

263. Each day I take time to imagine myself as a millionaire.

264. Feelings are creative, so I make the effort to feel like a lottery winner.

265. All my dreams are coming to pass thanks to the lottery.

266. I can easily handle a multi-million dollar lottery prize.

267. I have plenty of wealth to enjoy thanks to my lottery prize money.

268. I allow myself to manifest millions of dollars for my joy and pleasure.

269. There is no limit to the amount of money I can win.

270. My lottery prize money allows me to buy everything I want and need.

271. I am excited to help my family and friends with my millions of dollars.

272. I have always known that I would buy the winning ticket.

273. Positive energy constantly flows around me.

274. I emit a winning vibe.

275. I am aligned with the energy of money and abundance.

276. I cash in winning tickets all the time.

277. It's easy for me to win money.

278. I use my lottery millions to improve my life and the lives of others.

279. I am ready to enjoy a life of luxury.

280. I am confident in my ability to attract the winning ticket.

281. I am constantly visualizing myself as a multi-millionaire.

282. It's exciting to think about how much money I am about to win.

283. I intend to win a lottery jackpot this year.

284. I can already imagine the wonderful life I will have as a lottery winner.

285. I am about to win more money than I can ever spend.

286. I have the ability to be incredibly wealthy.

287. Every ticket I buy is a winner.

288. I am so excited to collect my lottery prize money.

289. I am financially free thanks to my lottery jackpot.

290. An avalanche of cash is about to appear in my life.

291. Being a lottery millionaire gives me the ability to support the causes I care about.

292. My life is filled with financial abundance thanks to my lottery win.

293. I create my own luck with the power of my spoken word.

294. I am enjoying a lifestyle of luxury thanks to my lottery millions.

295. I give thanks for my large, steady, and dependable annuity from the lottery.

296. Becoming a lottery millionaire is a priority for me.

297. I expect and receive money miracles all the time.

298. Every word I speak is in harmony with my desire to manifest millions of dollars.

299. My circumstances are changing, and money is flowing to me in great abundance.

300. I already know what house and car I will buy when I cash in my winning ticket.

If you enjoyed this book, please read my other books:

HOW TO WIN THE LOTTERY WITH THE LAW OF ATTRACTION: FOUR LOTTERY WINNERS SHARE THEIR MANIFESTATION TECHNIQUES

MANIFEST YOUR MILLIONS: A LOTTERY WINNER SHARES HIS LAW OF ATTRACTION SECRETS

ADVANCED LAW OF ATTRACTION TECHNIQUES: MASTERING MANIFESTATION AND ATTRACTING WHAT YOU WANT FAST!

THE POWER OF YOUR SPOKEN WORD: 300 POWERFUL AFFIRMATIONS FOR MANIFESTING MONEY AND MASSIVE SUCCESS

MANIFESTING LOVE: HOW TO ATTRACT YOUR SOUL MATE WITH THE LAW OF ATTRACTION

Made in the USA
Middletown, DE
20 August 2023